The Big Book of
Gazebos, Pergolas,
and Other Backyard Architecture

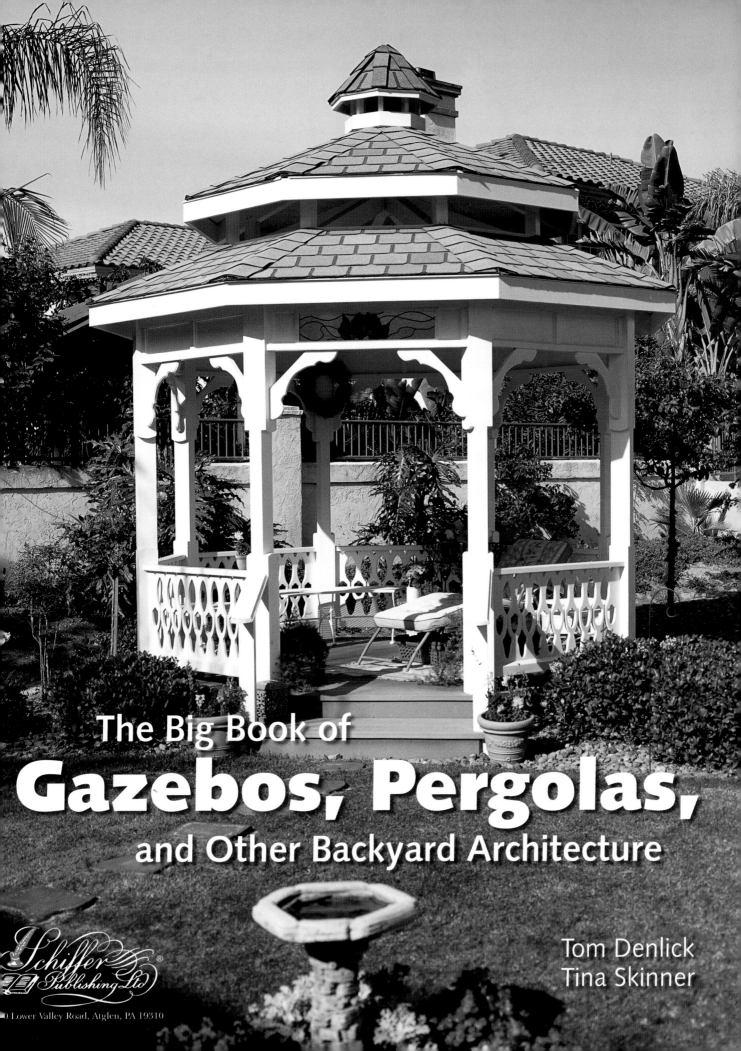

The Big Book of
Gazebos, Pergolas,
and Other Backyard Architecture

Tom Denlick
Tina Skinner

Schiffer Publishing Ltd

0 Lower Valley Road, Atglen, PA 19310

Other Schiffer Books by Tina Skinner
Garden Projects for the Backyard Carpenter. ISBN: 0764312340. $19.95
Outdoor Wood Works: With Complete Plans for Ten Projects. ISBN: 0764304461. $19.95

Other Schiffer Books on Related Subjects
The Deck Book: Inspirational Design Ideas. Melissa Cardona Hickory Dickory Decks. ISBN: 0764322842. $19.95

Copyright © 2009 by Tom Denlick & Schiffer Publishing
Library of Congress Control Number: 2008944386

Type set in University Roman Bd BT/Humanist 521 BT

ISBN: 978-0-7643-3170-1
Printed in China

Schiffer Books are available at special discounts for bulk purchases for sales promotions or premiums. Special editions, including personalized covers, corporate imprints, and excerpts can be created in large quantities for special needs. For more information contact the publisher:

Published by Schiffer Publishing Ltd.
4880 Lower Valley Road
Atglen, PA 19310
Phone: (610) 593-1777; Fax: (610) 593-2002
E-mail: Info@schifferbooks.com

For the largest selection of fine reference books on this and related subjects, please visit our web site at
www.schifferbooks.com
We are always looking for people to write books on new and related subjects. If you have an idea for a book please contact us at the above address.

This book may be purchased from the publisher.
Include $5.00 for shipping.
Please try your bookstore first.
You may write for a free catalog.

In Europe, Schiffer books are distributed by
Bushwood Books
6 Marksbury Ave.
Kew Gardens
Surrey TW9 4JF England
Phone: 44 (0) 20 8392 8585; Fax: 44 (0) 20 8392 9876
E-mail: info@bushwoodbooks.co.uk
Website: www.bushwoodbooks.co.uk

Contents

Introduction _____ 6
Why Build a Gazebo? _____ 7
   Quiet Escapes _____ 7
   Garden Focal Points _____ 28
   Garden Sheds _____ 36
   View Masters _____ 38
   Grand Entries _____ 54
   Outdoor Rooms _____ 56
   Party Places & Pavilions _____ 81
   Pool Houses _____ 89
   Spas _____ 96
Choosing a Design _____ 97
   Arbors _____ 97
   Pergolas _____ 108
   Multi-tiered Gazebos _____ 117
   Squares and Rectangles _____ 123
   Foreign Influence _____ 130
   Follies _____ 136
      Garden Tours _____ 137
Elements of Design _____ 147
   Cupolas _____ 147
   A Look Under the Hood _____ 148
   Frieze Panels _____ 152
   Corbels & Decorative Brackets _____ 154
   Railings & Panels _____ 155
   The Base _____ 161
Knowing the Language _____ 162
   A Glossary of Terms _____ 162
   Manufacturers & Contributors _____ 175

Introduction

There is something quite magical about a gazebo. Whether it's perched high on a hillside, tucked away in a private corner, or nestled in the middle of an English garden, gazebos seem to take on a unique charm. Defined as a freestanding, roofed, usually open-sided structure providing a shady resting place, "gazebo" comes from the French, meaning "to gaze to and from."

Your gazebo can become a small version of your own home by taking on your home's architectural features, or it can be designed with a more fanciful and gingerbread look. Whether in your backyard or in a park setting, landscape buildings such as gazebos, pergolas, or pavilions also provide structure to your space. As a garden amenity to sit in and look out from, it stands solid. It's unmovable, independent, unyielding, yet inviting. It marks its own boundaries. It gives one a feeling of security and peacefulness. It extends one's living quarters to the outdoors.

These structures can serve a specific function. They can enclose a spa, provide protection from the sun, or house a swing or hammock. Some have been used for art studios, changing rooms at poolsides, kiosks, or church information booths. A gazebo will not only provide a space for your landscape, but when roofed it provides shelter, and when enclosed it can become a detached room addition.

A gazebo, however, does not even have to be useful, it can be just for fun. It can be whimsical. It sets a tone and lends a mood to your yard. Everything can revolve around it becoming the hub of activity, or it can be private and hardly visible. A gazebo can often mirror the personality of its owner.

Brought to the Western world by Marco Polo in the thirteenth century, gazebos served as a meeting place for men to chat and smoke their pipes. During the Victorian era, gazebos took on a more romantic appeal, as they became meeting places for lovers.

Today, gazebos can be part of a landscape plan that includes a barbecue, pool, or an entire entertainment center with television and computer access. They are ideal for a luncheon, a children's playhouse, a wedding, or a band pavilion. Take advantage of a spectacular view by perching it on a hillside or over the edge of a cliff.

Size, shape, and style are other considerations. It may be small enough for just the two of you, or large enough for an entire orchestra. It can be square shaped, octagonal, hexagonal, or just about any configuration imaginable. The style can be simple or ornate from contemporary to Oriental, Victorian to Spanish.

Tom Denlick

Why Build a Gazebo?

Quiet Escapes

Building a backyard structure creates the opportunity to enjoy your own spa, your own quiet place to walk away from the chores, the ringing phone, and life's other cares. For a couple, it can be a place to reconnect, for children a place to escape into the imagination. The following structures and the settings inspire dreams of splendid isolation, and offer up lots of appealing features you might want to incorporate into your life, and your backyard setting.

Lattice walls create a sense of privacy for a gazebo, its handsome lead roof an ornament for an intimate outdoor gathering area. *Courtesy of HSP Garden Buildings*

A sloped lead roof lends its shimmer to a water-front setting. *Courtesy of HSP Garden Buildings*

A wooden bridge highlights the journey to a gazebo destination. *Courtesy of Leisure Designs*

A garden path leads to a gazebo, sheltered in the lea of a substantial privacy wall. *Courtesy of Leisure Designs*

A gazebo sits atop a hill, offering a view, but more importantly drawing people with the promise of an escape from the maddening crowd. *Courtesy of Leisure Designs*

Comfortable chairs, shade, and a sense of splendid isolation are parts of the enticement offered by this gazebo. *Courtesy of Leisure Designs*

A wind vane adds to the rural whimsy of a gazebo gracing a beautiful meadow. *Courtesy of Leisure Designs*

Stepping-stones wend their way around a small garden pond to the pinnacle attraction, a white gazebo. *Courtesy of Leisure Designs*

Red railing underlines a pretty roof, where tiles create a scalloped profile. *Courtesy of Leisure Designs*

Redwood finish adds to the nostalgic,
rustic nature of this gazebo set at
the terminus of a rock-lined path.
Courtesy of Leisure Designs

A shingled cupola adds stature
to an attractive structure.
Courtesy of Leisure Designs

An inviting swing is suspended from a decorative pergola, the perfect ending to a handsome garden path.
Courtesy of Leisure Designs

A gazebo, located in the corner of a backyard, creates a getaway far from the cares and chores of the home.
Courtesy of Leisure Designs

White wicker and painted wood add luster to the outdoors. *Courtesy of Leisure Designs*

Even with a sheltered patio close to the home, a gazebo gets visitors who want to get just a bit further from the daily cares. *Courtesy of Leisure Designs*

A triple-tiered gazebo crowns an outdoor party area, with a barbecue center and room to squeeze in a crowd should the weather go south. *Courtesy of Leisure Designs*

An enormous, three-tiered gazebo shown with and without Christmas decor. Installed lighting, with the addition of the twinkling light garlands, gives the structure an enticing nighttime glow. *Courtesy of Leisure Designs*

Comfortable furnishings and a fireplace for warm evenings embellish the interior of an expansive gazebo. *Courtesy of Leisure Designs*

A circular bench is poetically protected by a pretty gazebo, topped by a witch's hat roof. *Courtesy of HSP Garden Buildings*

A peaked roof caps an attractive bench, inviting even in sub-freezing temperatures. *Courtesy of HSP Garden Buildings*

Red and metallic, this romantic little getaway is an alluring garden ornament.
Courtesy of HSP Garden Buildings

With all the charm of a country garden, stepping-stones lead eye and feet alike to a pretty white gazebo. *Courtesy of Vixen Hill Gazebos*

A wooden gazebo is an irresistible resting place waterside. *Courtesy of Vixen Hill Gazebos*

Woodwork frames the columned openings in a white gazebo. *Courtesy of Vixen Hill Gazebos*

A two-tiered room crowns a small gazebo at the terminus of a catwalk. *Courtesy of Dalton Pavilions, Inc.*

A two-tiered gazebo overlooks an oceanfront view. *Courtesy of Dalton Pavilions, Inc.*

A bridge and a pretty gazebo are irresistible attractions. *Courtesy of Dalton Pavilions, Inc.*

A pretty garden house adds ornament to its setting. *Courtesy of HSP Garden Buildings*

This lovely little two-seater forms an outpost at the edge of the forest. *Courtesy of Dalton Pavilions, Inc.*

Lattice underlines an eight-sided shingle roof, a shelter for small groups seeking a handy escape. *Courtesy of Dalton Pavilions, Inc.*

A gazebo easily becomes another architectural element in the homeowner's landscape. *Courtesy of Dalton Pavilions, Inc.*

Iron hinges and scroll-cut balusters add beauty to a screened gazebo. *Courtesy of Dalton Pavilions, Inc.*

Open woodwork creates a lacy cap for an eight-sided garden getaway. *Courtesy of Dalton Pavilions, Inc.*

A little screened in gazebo creates a summer sanctuary, set at the periphery of the patio. *Courtesy of Dalton Pavilions, Inc.*

Seasonal ornaments adorn a much loved garden pavilion, visited even in the roughest of weather, and oft admired from behind frosted windows. *Courtesy of Dalton Pavilions, Inc.*

A weathervane and small cupola are creative caps for a roofline that delights in every way. *Courtesy of Dalton Pavilions, Inc.*

Curved balusters add interest to the railing surrounding a screened-in gazebo, and a medley of wood tones creates endless interest. *Courtesy of Dalton Pavilions, Inc.*

Latticework has a special magic when lit from within. *Courtesy of Dalton Pavilions, Inc.*

Outfitted for picnics, this pavilion is a destination in the garden. *Courtesy of Dalton Pavilions, Inc.*

Garden Focal Points

Despite all the care lavished on the greenery, and the fragile blooms of color a gardener coaxes from her floral charges, a beautiful garden structure is going to be the star of the scene. Whether rising above the garden, or bearing vines upon its timbers, the gazebo or pergola finds itself the focal point of a garden setting. Careful placement and tasteful design enhance the effect. Moreover, it's a sight to be enjoyed year round, whether covered with snow or falling leaves, creating a velvety pool of cooling shade on a lazy summer's afternoon, or simply basking in the glory of a garden during the height of spring.

The stepped pedestal of a gazebo becomes a pretty platform for a floral display.
Courtesy of Leisure Designs

Even within an extensive landscape, it is the architecture that is most eye-catching. A small gazebo is the crowning jewel in this colorful setting, it's impact echoed in stairwells and concrete railings that connect the space.
Courtesy of Leisure Designs

A stone patio terminates in a pretty gazebo, its red roof an ornament within the greenery. *Courtesy of Leisure Designs*

A grassy lawn is more inviting with a gazebo resting on it. *Courtesy of Leisure Designs*

A gazebo in the garden is skirted in flowers within a blanket of green.
Courtesy of Leisure Designs

Two treasures – an antique canon and a beloved gazebo – share star billing in a backyard.
Courtesy of Leisure Designs

A gazebo enhances a pool setting, creating a focal point, and offering an invitation for shelter and privacy. *Courtesy of Leisure Designs*

A desert garden setting is brightened by a gazebo. *Courtesy of Leisure Designs*

The gingerbread details of this gazebo help it compete with the lush setting it graces.
Courtesy of Leisure Designs

In a pretty landscape, replete with pool, flowering plants, and a scattering of stonework, the pavilion is undeniably the main attraction. *Courtesy of Amish Country Gazebos*

A lakeside gazebo displays curved planes on the exterior roofline, a barrel vault ceiling within. *Courtesy of Dalton Pavilions, Inc.*

Snow caps a wooden yard ornament. *Courtesy of Dalton Pavilions, Inc.*

A perfect, pretty blue bench adds delightful ornament to a cottage garden setting. *Courtesy of HSP Garden Buildings*

The utility of a bench is almost lost under the awe of a pointed arch, capped by a finial. *Courtesy of HSP Garden Buildings*

Garden Sheds

A structure within the garden needn't be just ornamental. Alternately, a shed for garden tools can also be ornamental. Following are a couple of wonderful examples of structures that might help hide the messier aspects of maintaining an amazing landscape while adding to the overall appearance.

Brick wall is repeated on the facade of a folly, with Ionic columns capped by a pediment.
Courtesy of Haddonstone

A purple garden house sits conservatory-like; appropriately grand in relation to the home it was paired with.
Courtesy of HSP Garden Buildings

View Masters

A great view begs the viewer to linger. Building a shrine to a great outlook seems only logical. Here are examples of gazebos and pavilions that make visitors masters of all they survey.

A gazebo creates an inviting vantage for an impressive view.
Courtesy of Leisure Designs

A lattice roof illuminates a pretty, hilltop gazebo. *Courtesy of Leisure Designs*

The irresistible draw of an expansive view is made all that much more attractive when a place is provided from which to enjoy it. *Courtesy of Leisure Designs*

A Plexiglas railing and partial sides for this gazebo help shelter it from the winds that are part and parcel of enjoying an incredible view. *Courtesy of Leisure Designs*

A geometric railing adds ornament to a gazebo overlooking the park.
Courtesy of Leisure Designs

A decorative concrete platform underlines a gazebo with a great overlook. *Courtesy of Leisure Designs*

Latticework creates the icing on a hilltop gazebo.
Courtesy of Leisure Designs

A backyard drops off steeply, but you're drawn to the edge nonetheless, where a gazebo serves up a view. *Courtesy of Leisure Designs*

An expansive gazebo sits on the hilltop, commanding the view. *Courtesy of Leisure Designs*

A green metal roof caps pristine white metal framing on a lakefront gazebo. *Courtesy of Icon Shelter Systems, Inc.*

A deck structure forms an outpost at the periphery of a lawn. *Courtesy of Leisure Designs*

A massive stone pillar lofts a gazebo above the water. *Courtesy of Vixen Hill Gazebos*

Posts support a gazebo elevated to the level of a deck. *Courtesy of Vixen Hill Gazebos*

A dome-roofed gazebo crowns a small platform, buttressed by a stone retaining wall. *Courtesy of HSP Garden Buildings*

Window grids turn a gazebo into an enclosed room for this watery location. *Courtesy of Vixen Hill Gazebos*

Benches encircle a
two-tiered gazebo
with an expansive view.
*Courtesy of Vixen Hill
Gazebos*

A petite gazebo adds a shady respite near a tropical beach. *Courtesy of Vixen Hill Gazebos*

Glowing from within, a tiered gazebo becomes the view by night, master of the view by day.
Courtesy of Amish Country Gazebos

Within the setting of the great outdoors, an architectural element defines gathering places to help bring people together.
Courtesy of Dalton Pavilions, Inc.

A gazebo gives vantage to a view. *Courtesy of Dalton Pavilions, Inc.*

Folks on land and water alike benefit from the addition of a pretty gazebo on the shore. *Courtesy of Dalton Pavilions, Inc.*

A gazebo is the literal cornerstone of a raised patio. Set atop a retaining wall, it actually caps a lower storage level. On the patio level, a two-tiered roof floods the interior with light and inspiring beauty. *Courtesy of McHale Landscape Design, Inc.*

Grand Entries

Like a front door or an entry foyer, a garden's entryway is an important part of creating a first impression. Following are stylish ideas for adding architecture to the eye candy you create in your landscape.

Stone columns define a passageway through a matching wall, and support an appropriately massive sixteen-foot bell roof. *Courtesy of Dalton Pavilions, Inc.*

A pavilion serves as a passageway, or pausing point, along a garden path. *Courtesy of Dalton Pavilions, Inc.*

A trellis-topped gate adds ornament to a garden walkway, serving more as an invitation than a barrier.
Courtesy of Trellis Structures

An arbor creates a passageway amidst a formal garden's paths. *Courtesy of Trellis Structures*

Outdoor Rooms

The hottest trend in home design and improvement today is actually taking place behind the home. Americans are investing like never before in their backyards, creating open-air living spaces that include kitchen appliances and fireplaces. The traditional picnic table and lawn chairs have gotten a major upgrade, too. Following are wonderful examples of projects that indulge their owners' desire to spend more time outdoors.

A party pavilion is an important room in the home, an invitation to gather in all clement weather. Within, a full kitchen makes cooking outside completely convenient. *Courtesy of McHale Landscape Design, Inc.*

Classical columns support an open roof capping a fire lit outdoor dining area. *Courtesy of The Outdoor Greatroom Company*

The living room moves outdoor with the addition of a fireplace, a cook center, and pergola to define an area where folks can gather and relax within the wide expanse of outdoors. *Courtesy of The Outdoor Greatroom Company*

An arched pergola forms an extension
of the home. A propane-fueled table
proffers fire in civilized style to create
a centerpiece for intimate gatherings.
*Courtesy of The Outdoor Greatroom
Company*

An arched pergola adds loft and definition to an outdoor living room, warmed by fire. *Courtesy of The Outdoor Greatroom Company*

A trellised space forms a magnet at the back of the yard, anchored by a massive stone fireplace. *Courtesy of McHale Landscape Design, Inc.*

A brick back wall and foursquare columns add architectural permanence and establishment to this backyard setting. *Courtesy of McHale Landscape Design, Inc.*

A fireplace forms the terminus
for a columned outdoor room.
*Courtesy of The Outdoor Greatroom
Company*

The beautiful wood tones of a pergola add warmth to an impressive backyard designed with entertaining in mind. *Courtesy of McHale Landscape Design, Inc.*

A trellis roof defines an outdoor living space, outfitted with barbecue center and a fireplace. *Courtesy of McHale Landscape Design, Inc.*

A cupola crowns the square roof of a poolside gazebo. A kitchen and dining area make it possible for a family to spend the bulk of their free summer hours outdoors. *Courtesy of McHale Landscape Design, Inc.*

An outdoor living room is all about convenience. A gas fireplace fires up on demand, making it easy to squeeze in an hour relaxing amidst a busy schedule. *Courtesy of McHale Landscape Design, Inc.*

Gingerbread cutouts given lace-like trim to arched openings in this expansive screened gazebo. *Courtesy of Vixen Hill Gazebos*

A screened gazebo casts a golden glow, from its red and yellow wood finishes to the copper roof. *Courtesy of Vixen Hill Gazebos*

A gazebo angles around a patio area, sheltering a full kitchen and outdoor living area. A handsome fireplace of stacked ashlar stone warms the seating area. In the kitchen area, an eating counter fronts the wet bar area, while a cooking center flanks the back wall. Televised entertainment is broadcast both above the fireplace and from a mounted screen that faces the kitchen. *Courtesy of Neals Design-Remodel*

A square pergola caps a neat brick patio area. *Courtesy of Vixen Hill Gazebos*

The interior of an octagonal gazebo is a showcase for wood artistry, with floor and ceiling tracing the pleasing shape, and latticework forming a sparkling frame for the views. *Courtesy of Dalton Pavilions, Inc.*

A living room setting fits nicely within a thirteen-foot gazebo. A ceiling fan adds to summer comfort levels. *Courtesy of Dalton Pavilions, Inc.*

Retractable screens provide access to breeze, or cut off access to irritating pests. *Courtesy of Dalton Pavilions, Inc.*

Lattice and home add walls to two sides of a trellised deck. *Courtesy of Trellis Structures*

A white pergola defines a space dedicated to relaxing fireside. *Courtesy of Trellis Structures*

Like a folding screen in the home, a three-part trellis helps create a sense of space and privacy, an airy kind of wall. Unlike a wall inside the home, though, it frames a view instead of holding frames of views. *Courtesy of Arboria Products*

A four-part screen creates a border for a patio area, and creates a barrier against casual trespass. *Courtesy of Arboria Products*

Party Places & Pavilions

For those who entertain often, moving the party outdoors is an attractive option. A pavilion is a wonderful solution for areas frequently host to rain, but open air spaces work well, too. Following are ideas for creating spaces where people will naturally congregate within the expanse of a landscape.

A gazebo stretches under two tiers of roof, adorned with gingerbread woodwork in high Victorian style.
Courtesy of Amish Country Gazebos

Crisp white woodwork, costumes, and parasols hark back to Victorian times, and emphasize the enduring popularity of the gazebo in outdoor celebrations. *Courtesy of Leisure Designs*

Red tile puts this gazebo squarely in its western setting. A barbecue makes grilling up lunch an easy task and a natural draw. *Courtesy of Leisure Designs*

A gazebo adorns its garden, tent-like with its sloped roof and draped sides. Half of the structure stands open atop slender columns while the latter half provides concealment for storage and off-weather entertaining. *Courtesy of HSP Garden Buildings*

A garden room provides the perfect place to push spring forward a month or two. *Courtesy of HSP Garden Buildings*

Beacon-like, a cupola crowns a gazebo and evokes a sense of heritage alongside an American flag. *Courtesy of Icon Shelter Systems, Inc.*

A cloth pavilion creates a sense of event in the backyard, while sheltering a permanent room complete with a brick fireplace and comfortable furnishings. *Courtesy of Kleeman & Associates Design Group*

Eight planes of a roof slope gracefully to rest on classic columns. *Courtesy of Dalton Pavilions, Inc.*

A tile roof adds Spanish flair to a gazebo. *Courtesy of Amish Country Gazebos*

A double-roofed pavilion is encircled by shrubbery and pea gravel. *Courtesy of Dalton Pavilions, Inc.*

A eight-sided, bell-shaped roof adds character to these two enclosed gazebos. *Courtesy of HSP Garden Buildings*

Pool Houses

Floaties, chlorine buckets, lounge chairs, towels, and other poolside accouterments find a home in stylish architecture in the following examples. A pool house might be small enough only to accommodate these needs, or expanded to provide a changing area, or even a shady spot where swimmers can escape the sun between dips.

An enclosed gazebo was outfitted with hinged double doors that fold open to reveal the better part of the interior to the pool setting beyond.
Courtesy of HSP Garden Buildings

A small spire caps an octagonal roof that rises atop a cupcake-like decoration on this attractive little lakefront platform. *Courtesy of HSP Garden Buildings*

A shingle-roofed gazebo offers a poolside shelter. Paneled walls bring tradition and beauty to the outdoor room. *Courtesy of Leisure Designs*

Tile adds profile to a gazebo roof and cupola. *Courtesy of Leisure Designs*

A gazebo crowns a platform that extends to the edge of a pool. *Courtesy of Leisure Designs*

Three tiers of roof crown a beautiful wooden screened gazebo. *Courtesy of Vixen Hill Gazebos*

A poolside gazebo is crowned by a raised cap that allows heat to vent from the structure's roof. *Courtesy of Leisure Designs*

White woodwork underlines a sloped, eight-sided roof. *Courtesy of Dalton Pavilions, Inc.*

A hexagonal roost provides a poolside perch. *Courtesy of Leisure Designs*

A manufactured gazebo is the instant answer to a need for a pool house. *Courtesy of Dalton Pavilions, Inc.*

Sun worshipping is out because of health concerns, so shade by the pool is desirable. *Courtesy of Dalton Pavilions, Inc.*

Classic columns frame the terminus of a pool and support a shelter for comfortable seating. *Courtesy of Dalton Pavilions, Inc.*

Spas

Whether to shelter it, or simply to provide a frame for a
prized spa, a structure makes a nice backyard addition.

A gazebo shelters a spa, protecting this relaxing treasure from the elements while allowing the owners to
enjoy it out of doors. *Courtesy of Leisure Designs*

A pergola provides a structure for a raised deck dedicated to a built-in spa.
Courtesy of Leisure Designs

Choosing a Design

Arbors

An arbor is an open framework that supports climbing plants. Often these are small archways, but they can be extended to create shaded walkways, seating areas, and garden focal points. The majority of these pictures were taken immediately after construction, so the planting is left up to your imagination, while the framework is detailed so that you can emulate it.

Porthole-like windows frame the brief view as one passes through this detailed arbor. *Courtesy of Trellis Structures*

A classic garden arbor design. *Courtesy of Arboria Products*

A trellised gateway is a pretty garden accent. *Courtesy of Arboria Products*

Round windows add punctuation to a trellis design. *Courtesy of Arboria Products*

A slatted roof provides shelter from the sun, with bench seating below. *Courtesy of Leisure Designs*

An arbor gateway creates a romantic divider in a garden setting. *Courtesy of Leisure Designs*

Climbing plants can be an integral part of the architecture, as shown here in this green arbor sheltering a barbecue center. *Courtesy of Leisure Designs*

An arbor rises above its lush surroundings. *Courtesy of Leisure Designs*

An arbor entryway to a garden was lavished with love and craftsmanship, from the paneled gate to the slatted arch overhead. *Courtesy of Leisure Designs*

Double columns mark the corners of a garden pergola. *Courtesy of Trellis Structures*

Lattice forms a backdrop for a columned pergola. *Courtesy of Trellis Structures*

It would be a shame to train climbing plants to cover this pretty little arbor, which forms a dominant element in a formal garden. *Courtesy of Trellis Structures*

Trellis defines a walkway and observation area for the tennis courts beyond. *Courtesy of Trellis Structures*

An expansive pergola provides an architectural element to a harsh winter landscape. In the summer, it provides a gathering space for large parties. *Courtesy of Trellis Structures*

Trellis work caps a colonnade that defines a lower patio area. *Courtesy of Trellis Structures*

Carefully proportioned in three parts, a trellised structure adds classical punctuation to a pool space.
Courtesy of Trellis Structures

A colonnade forms an arched attraction. *Courtesy of Dalton Pavilions, Inc.*

A curved pergola forms a crescent shadow for seating at the periphery of a patio. *Courtesy of Icon Shelter Systems, Inc.*

Pergolas

A pergola is, technically, an open structure. It may shade a patio or a walkway, and it may or may not be used to train climbing plants. Pergolas are a wonderful way to create the illusion of enclosure without sacrificing connection to the outdoors.

The exposed beams and cross rails of a pergola do more than provide that restful dappled shade.
They also provide endless opportunities for hanging things – plants, lighting, birdhouses, ...
Courtesy of American Building Products

A pergola provides a gathering point on the rocky shores of a lake. *Courtesy of McHale Landscape Design, Inc.*

White trelliswork forms a poetic frame for the sky, anchored by terra cotta tile. A stone fireplace is perfectly framed within the outline of the latticework. *Courtesy of Neals Design-Remodel*

Square fluted columns create a classical base for a pretty pergola roof. *Courtesy of Leisure Designs*

A pergola adds an outdoor room to its mission-style home. *Courtesy of Leisure Designs*

A pergola expands the living space behind the home, defining a new space where family activities can take place.
Courtesy of American Building Products

A pergola extends a shady area from the home, overlooked by a gazebo that acts as a draw further out in the yard. *Courtesy of Leisure Designs*

White picket fence and a matching pergola add architecture to this backyard, and improve the view from a wonderful bank of windows and sliding glass doors. *Courtesy of American Building Products*

A rounded edge adds beauty to a pergola designed to shelter shade plants in an exposed backyard. *Courtesy of American Building Products*

An open pergola sits poolside.
Courtesy of American Building Products

Eight handsome columns
line up to support a pergola.
*Courtesy of Dalton Pavilions,
Inc.*

A generous portion of white icing crowns a wonderful stone patio.
Courtesy of Trellis Structures

Multi-tiered Gazebos

Like the pagodas of the East, Western style gazebos tend to rise in layers, creating an impressive profile for the landscape.

A three-tiered roof rises above a jumble of beloved plants, flowers, and sculpture, creating a central focal point among many.
Courtesy of Leisure Designs

A garden gazebo rises to a crowning cupola, sitting cupcake-like in a backyard setting. *Courtesy of Leisure Designs*

Gingerbread provides a delicate underline for a three-tiered roof crown. *Courtesy of Leisure Designs*

A decorative roof creates architectural ornament within the site of future landscaping.
Courtesy of Leisure Designs

Glass windows and a space heater allow the owners to enjoy their little gazebo year round. *Courtesy of Vixen Hill Gazebos*

A gazebo can double as a fort; with a little imagination, it might even fly. *Courtesy of Vixen Hill Gazebos*

A gazebo shot in autumn glow. *Courtesy of Vixen Hill Gazebos*

A cupola tops three tiers of roofline on a handsome, pagoda-like pavilion. *Courtesy of Dalton Pavilions, Inc.*

The three tiers in this pavilion's roofline evoke pagodas of the Orient. *Courtesy of Dalton Pavilions, Inc.*

Squares and Rectangles

Most gazebos are six or eight sided. It seemed worthwhile to pull out samplings of those that break the mold, being built along straight lines.

A distinctive roof ridge and a textured cornice add distinction to a rectangular, poolside pavilion.
Courtesy of Leisure Designs

Four square pillars support the tile roof of a pavilion, set poolside. *Courtesy of Leisure Designs*

Classical appeal is created using a symmetrical, four-fronted design for a pavilion of distinction. *Courtesy of Leisure Designs*

Unfinished wood enhances the rustic appeal of a square pavilion. *Courtesy of Leisure Designs*

A square pavilion is set back from the pool, creating an alcove of sorts. Plexiglas dividers create wind and sound barriers, while keeping the view open. *Courtesy of Leisure Designs*

A four-sided pavilion overlooks a pool setting, shaded by tropical palm trees. *Courtesy of Leisure Designs*

An expansive pavilion creates a congregation spot, warmed by a massive fireplace.
Courtesy of Leisure Designs

A pavilion shelters a hot tub and creates a bar for beverages near an outdoor barbecue center.
Courtesy of Leisure Designs

Triple columns man each corner of a rectangular roofed gazebo. *Courtesy of Dalton Pavilions, Inc.*

Foreign Influence

A touch of the exotic is always welcome when daydreaming in the garden. Here are samples of structures that transport you to another time and place.

Asia influenced this wonderful, hilltop gazebo. *Courtesy of Leisure Designs*

A bell-shaped roof evokes European influences. *Courtesy of Leisure Designs*

A bell-shaped roof caps a poolside gazebo. *Courtesy of Leisure Designs*

Open roof slats make this structure a pergola, and add to its fanciful charm. *Courtesy of Leisure Designs*

Victorian tastes are emulated in turned balusters in the railing and detailed corbels supporting the roof.
Courtesy of Leisure Designs

Red tiles recall the Mediterranean rooftops that crowd hillside towns. *Courtesy of Leisure Designs*

A gazebo, topped by Spanish-style tiles, and underlined in pavers of like hue, extend the home into the outdoors. *Courtesy of Leisure Designs*

Red railing and roof add a distinctly California Revival feel to a pretty white gazebo.
Courtesy of Leisure Designs

Tile creates an impressive crown for a garden gazebo. *Courtesy of Leisure Designs*

An orange stain creates an Asian sensibility for this pergola. *Courtesy of Trellis Structures*

An open roofline adds wings to classic Tuscan columns. *Courtesy of Trellis Structures*

Follies

Follies are just that – something built simply for fun. The classic gardens of Europe often feature follies that are miniatures of famous temples or ruins. The function of these architectural gems is simply their ability to delight.

A classic is revived in an architectural folly that recreates Diana's temple in garden scale. *Courtesy of Haddonstone*

A balustraded gazebo creates an architectural folly at the periphery of a large lawn. *Courtesy of Haddonstone*

Garden Tour

The Folly Garden at The Gardens at Matterhorn features fantasy garden buildings from England that add a sudden and unexpected encounter while walking through the garden. Inspired by Gothic architecture and Olde English masonry, the Folly Garden was designed to provide a fresh and exciting palette of ideas for home landscape design. Following is your own personalized tour.

A recreated ruin caps a rocky hill, creating an intriguing focal point that beckons to explorers. *Courtesy of The Gardens at Matterhorn*

A fireplace appears to be a remnant of a former home, but it's also an active attraction for outdoor entertaining. *Courtesy of The Gardens at Matterhorn*

A fountain quietly refreshes beneath an open canopy of wood trellis. *Courtesy of The Gardens at Matterhorn*

Stone and brick end abruptly, and make way for tree limbs, in a fanciful nook created in sheer folly.
Courtesy of The Gardens at Matterhorn

Stone arches stand as a faux remnant of a previous gazebo. A matching archway forms a gate in the background.
Courtesy of The Gardens at Matterhorn

Passageways through rock follies create transitions within a garden setting, and stimulate the imagination.
These fanciful works of masonry art are year-round attractions, solid points within an ever-changing landscape.
Courtesy of The Gardens at Matterhorn

A well bubbles up in the center of a rustic pavilion. The sloping, shingled roof adds an innocent aspect to the shelter, and the charming railing was fashioned from branches intertwined and anchored for a primitive, cottage look.
Courtesy of The Gardens at Matterhorn

A trellised colonnade forms a vantage point pond side, creating a walkway to be relished.
Courtesy of The Gardens at Matterhorn

A lengthy trellis forms a framework for an expansive formal garden and patio area.
Courtesy of The Gardens at Matterhorn

Sloped corners accentuate the planes of an ornamental gazebo that marks the intersection of garden paths.
Courtesy of The Gardens at Matterhorn

A stone folly recreates Greek classicism in all its glory, atop a ceremonial font full of blooming lilies. *Courtesy of The Gardens at Matterhorn*

A trellis is part of the subtle charm in a petite patio setting, with potted plants and a wall fountain. *Courtesy of The Gardens at Matterhorn*

A small arbor was dedicated to the enjoyment of a favorite pet, offering shade on sunny summer days. *Courtesy of The Gardens at Matterhorn*

The crossed rafters of a pergola evoke a Finnish sensibility for this little garden respite. *Courtesy of The Gardens at Matterhorn*

A simple trellised entry-way adds focus and joy to a wintry landscape. *Courtesy of The Gardens at Matterhorn*

The ability to enjoy an amazing view is preserved against all possible weather with a sheltered gazebo. Within, under-counter cabinetry contains provisions that make it easy to extend the stay. *Courtesy of The Gardens at Matterhorn*

Corinthian columns support an open trellis, a pretty element in a well-loved garden. *Courtesy of The Gardens at Matterhorn*

Elements of Design

Cupolas

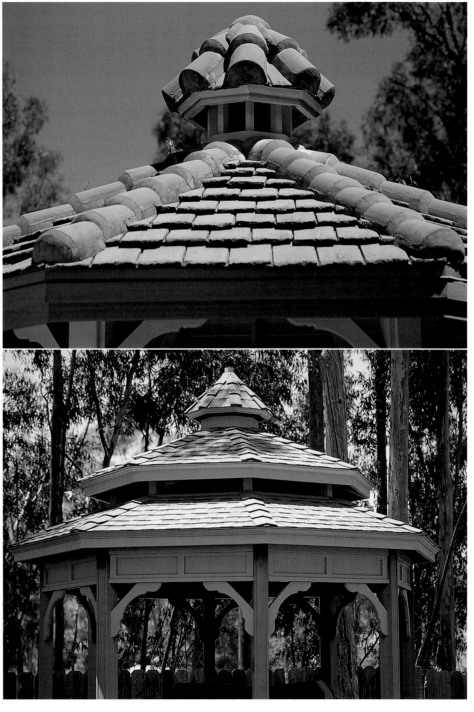

Courtesy of Leisure Designs

A Look Under the Hood

Courtesy of Leisure Designs

Courtesy of Leisure Designs

Courtesy of Leisure Designs

Courtesy of Leisure Designs

Courtesy of Leisure Designs

The interior of a two-tiered roof. *Courtesy of Dalton Pavilions, Inc.*

A barrel vault ceiling. *Courtesy of Dalton Pavilions, Inc.*

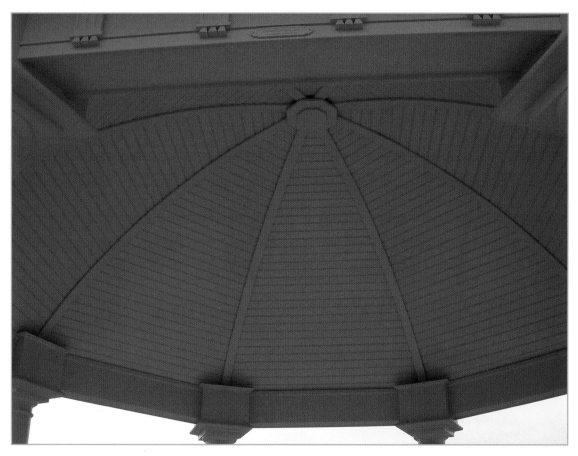

A detail of woodwork inside a barrel vault ceiling. *Courtesy of Dalton Pavilions, Inc.*

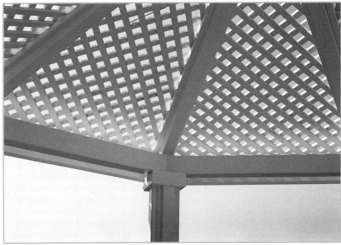

Wood tones adorn a hexagonal ceiling. *Courtesy of Dalton Pavilions, Inc.*

Looking up at a sunny sky through the latticed roof of a pergola. *Courtesy of Leisure Designs*

The wooden framework of the roof is highlighted above the white framework of the base. *Courtesy of Dalton Pavilions, Inc.*

Frieze Panels

Courtesy of Leisure Designs

Courtesy of Leisure Designs

Courtesy of Leisure Designs

*Courtesy of Leisure
Designs*

*Courtesy of Leisure
Designs*

*Courtesy of Leisure
Designs*

Corbels & Decorative Brackets

Courtesy of Leisure Designs

Courtesy of Leisure Designs

Courtesy of Leisure Designs

Courtesy of Leisure Designs

Courtesy of Leisure Designs

Courtesy of Leisure Designs

Courtesy of Leisure Designs

Courtesy of Leisure Designs

Courtesy of Leisure Designs

Courtesy of Leisure Designs

Courtesy of Leisure Designs

Courtesy of Leisure Designs

Courtesy of Leisure Designs

Courtesy of Leisure Designs

Courtesy of Leisure Designs

The Base

Built-in benches eliminate the need to furnish a gazebo. *Courtesy of Dalton Pavilions, Inc.*

A concrete floor is an easy maintenance option for a new gazebo. *Courtesy of Dalton Pavilions, Inc.*

Pretty turned posts support the tile roof of this gazebo. The structure sits atop a raised platform, buttressed by stone and surfaced with brick pavers. *Courtesy of Leisure Designs*

Knowing the Terms

Glossary

Acute arch: An arch with two centers of curvature that are outside its span, resulting in a severely pointed form. See **two-centered arch**.

Arbor: A arrangement of intertwined trees, shrubs, or vines supported by a latticed frame, often forming an outdoor arch or passageway.

Hydrangea overwhelms a rustic arbor at the height of their bloom. When they die back, a pretty passageway will continue to adorn this little stopping point. *Courtesy of The Gardens at Matterhorn*

Arboretum: A botanical garden in which trees are displayed for scientific or educational purposes.

Arcade: A line of arches supported by columns, sometimes in conjunction with a covered walkway.

Arch: A curved construction spanning an opening, composed of wedge-shaped blocks, which translates weight from above onto vertical supports on each side. Arches take a variety of shapes, from semicircular to semi-elliptical to pointed.

Architecture: The science, art, and profession of designing and constructing buildings or other structures, in accordance with the principles of function and style.

Architrave: The beam resting immediately upon the capital of a column, and spanning from one column to another. Also, the decorative moldings enhancing the lintel and jambs of a doorway or window.

A colonnade supports beams extending from the house. *Courtesy of Haddonstone*

Architrave cornice: An entablature in which the frieze is omitted, allowing the cornice to rest directly on the architrave.

Arch order: An arch set within columns and an entablature or another arch.

Archway: A passageway or entrance under an arch.

Art Deco: An architectural and decorative style popularized in the 1920s and '30s, characterized by angular or zigzag forms and patterns.

Art Nouveau: Movement in art and architecture in the late nineteenth century that stressed organic and dynamic forms and curvilinear designs.

Arts and Crafts: Aesthetic movement in Europe and America during the late nineteenth century which sought high standards of design and craftsmanship in everyday objects and architecture. Characteristics of Arts and Crafts architecture include low-pitched roofs, exposed rafters under eaves, and the use of mixed materials.

Ashlar: Squared building stone.

Ashlar brick, or rock-faced brick: A brick cut to resemble rough-hewn stone. See **ashlar**.

Bargeboard, gableboard, vergeboard: A board hanging from the projecting end of a roof so as to cover a portion of the gable.

Barge couple: The two rafters supporting an overhanging gable roof.

Barred-and-braced gate: A gate whose horizontal rails are reinforced by a diagonal brace.

Barred gate: A gate with horizontal timber rails.

Barrel arch: An arch constructed with a single curved slab.

Barrel vault: A vault with an arched, semi-circular ceiling.

A barrel roof crowns a spacious pavilion. *Courtesy of Vixen Hill Gazebos*

Base (columns): The bottom part of a column, resting on the plinth, and taking a variety of shapes and forms.

Belvedere: A rooftop structure, also called a gazebo, from which a view can be enjoyed.

Botanical garden: A garden containing a variety of plants, especially for scientific study.

Cairn: A landmark, monument, or memorial composed of piled stones.

Capital: The topmost portion of a column.

Capitals crown three columns on the corner of a gazebo. *Courtesy of Dalton Pavilions, Inc.*

Casement: A window sash with hinges that allow it to swing open along its length.

Cincture: Molding around the top or bottom of a column separating the capital or base from the shaft.

Circular arch: Arch with an interior curve that forms a segment of a circle.

A circular arch. *Courtesy of Arboria Products*

Classical architecture: The architecture of Hellenic Greece and Imperial Rome, characterized by the five classical orders.

Classical order: Any of the five styles of columns and their corresponding entablatures, as featured in classical Greek and Roman architecture. These include the Doric, Ionic, and Corinthian orders from the Greek, and the Tuscan and Composite orders from the Roman.

Classicism: Architectural principles stressing the correct use of Greek, Roman, and Italian renaissance forms.

Classic Revival: A return to classical Greek and Roman forms which arose in Europe and the United States during the early nineteenth century.

Clerestory: High-set window in a room with tall ceilings, positioned so as to let light into its center.

Cloister: A covered walk enclosing a courtyard, usually associated with monasteries or other ecclesiastical buildings.

Clustered Column: A group of columns connected to form a single structural element.

Collar beam: A horizontal beam tying together two oppositional rafters, generally positioned half-way up the rafters.

Collar beam roof: A roof constructed with collar beams. See **collar beam**.

Collar brace: Structural brace reinforcing a **collar beam**.

Colonnade: A row of columns supporting an entablature.

A colonnade is a series of columns arranged at intervals called intercolumniation, supporting an entablature and, sometimes, one side of a roof. The architrave is the beam resting upon the capital of the column. *Courtesy of Haddonstone*

Column: A long, slender, load-bearing structural element such as a post, pillar, or strut.

Common ashlar: A block of stone hewn with pick or hammer.

Common rafter: A rafter running from the eaves to the ridge of a roof.

Conservatory: A room or building, enclosed in glass, for the purpose of collecting and cultivating plants.

Console: a bracket braced against a wall to form support for a cornice, door, or window head.

Decorative brackets, or consoles, support the juncture of roof and column. *Courtesy of Leisure Designs*

Corinthian: One of the three Greek orders, characterized by a bell-shaped capital decorated with ornately carved acanthus leaves, and an elaborate cornice.

Corner post: A post placed at a corner in timber construction, to which other boards are nailed.

Coupled columns: Columns arranged in close pairs.

Coupled windows: A pair of closely spaced windows.

Coupled roof: A double-pitched roof with a narrow span and rafters that are not tied together.

Coursed ashlar: Ashlar masonry in which each individual course contains stones of uniform height, although all the courses are not necessarily the same height.

Coursed masonry: Construction in which stones are laid in regular courses.

Coursed rubble: Construction in which irregularly sized and shaped stones are stacked without courses, with mortar and smaller stones filling the gaps between them.

Court, Courtyard: Open area surrounded fully or partially by buildings or other walls.

Crest: A finial or ornament above a roof, wall, or other structure.

Cross vault: A vault formed by two **barrel vaults** intersecting at right angles.

Crown: The top of an arch or the corona of a cornice, often ornately decorated.

Crown molding: A molding serving as the finishing section of a structure.

Cupola: A circular-based dome set on the ridge of a roof.

An open cupola caps an eight-sided lath roof. *Courtesy of Dalton Pavilions, Inc.*

Curb roof: A roof sloping away from the ridge in two planes, also called a gambrel or mansard roof.

Cusp: The figure formed when two arcs intersect in a tracery.

Cusped arch: An arch incorporating cusps on its interior curve.

Dentil: A small "tooth," or square block, repeated to form the typical ornamentation in the Ionic, Corinthian, and Composite orders of classical architecture.

Depressed arch: An arch with two centers of curvature that are within its span, resulting in a blunt pointed form.

Doric: One of the three Greek orders, characterized by sturdy columns with a simple capital and base.

Dormer: A structure extending perpendicularly from a sloping roof.

Dormer window: A window, encased in a small dormer, projecting from a sloping roof.

Double window: see **coupled window**.

Dripping eaves: Eaves projecting beyond the wall, allowing water from the roof to fall to the ground without a gutter.

White woodwork contrasts with the darker areas in the two-tiered roofline. *Courtesy of Dalton Pavilions, Inc.*

Dutch gable: A gable with multi-carved sides and a vertically projecting pediment.

Eastlake style: An aesthetic movement of the Victorian period, characterized by rich ornamentation and heavy brackets.

Eaves: The lower portion of a sloping roof.

Eaves channel: A small gutter running along the top of a wall, leading to spouts for rainwater.

Edge shafts: Shafts supporting arches and connected to a nearby wall, giving the impression that they support only their edge.

Elevation: A drawing depicting the vertical elements of a building.

Elliptical arch: An arch taking the shape of a semi-ellipse.

Embedded column: A column set partially into a wall.

Embellishment: decoration.

Emboss: to indent a pattern into a material, creating a depression or raised area in the final product.

Entablature: The beam supported by the columns in classical architecture, composed of the **architrave**, the **frieze**, and the **cornice**.

Epistyle: The architrave.

Equilateral arch: A two-centered arch whose centers of curvature are separated by a distance equal the span of the arch.

Espalier: A trellis on which a tree's branches are spread vertically to form a single plane, or a tree grown in this fashion.

Esplanade: An open space for driving or walking.

Eye: The center of a circular pattern or ornament, as in those adorning Ionic columns.

Façade: The exterior front of an edifice.

Facing: A layer of decorative material over less-attractive structural materials.

Finial: An ornament marking the highest point, such as a spire.

An acorn-shaped ornament crowns the roof of a pavilion. *Courtesy of Dalton Pavilions, Inc.*

The roofline follows the curve of an elliptical arch. Louvered shutters add an interesting option for privacy to this otherwise open pergola. *Courtesy of The Outdoor Greatroom Company*

Flute: a decorative channel carved into the shaft of a column or other structure.

Fluting: ornamentation involving a series of flutes.

Folly: A purely ornamental structure, sometimes taking the form of a false ruin or a miniature, neo-classical structure.

A classic is revived in an architectural folly that recreate Diana's temple in garden scale. *Courtesy of Haddonstone*

Formal garden: A geometrically designed garden with a definite, symmetrical form.

Four-centered arch: An arch with four centers of curvature, producing a pointed, semi-elliptical shape.

Framing: The structural woodwork of a building, often consisting of rough timbers.

French roof: A **mansard** roof with sloping sides that are nearly perpendicular.

French window: A **casement** window extending all the way to the floor.

Fret: A decoration composed of continuous lines arranged in rectilinear forms, often above or surrounding a frieze or mosaic.

Fretwork: Any decorative openwork or interlaced work that is highly detailed and set in relief.

Gable: The vertical part of the end of a building, revealing a cross-view of the roof from the eaves to the ridge.

Gableboard: See **bargeboard**.

Gabled tower: A tower terminating in two or more gables, as opposed to a spire.

Gable end: An end wall with a gable.

Gable roof: A roof with a gable on at least one end.

Gable wall: A wall topped by a gable.

Gable window: A window set in a gable.

Gallery: A long, covered corridor on the interior or exterior of a building, or stretching between structures.

Gambrel roof: A roof with two pitches on each side, the lower being steeper than the upper.

Gateway: An opening in a fence or wall, or the ornamentation surrounding this opening.

An exciting arts and crafts motif was incorporated into this fence railing with matching gate and trellised archway. *Courtesy of Trellis Structures*

Gauged arch: An arch composed of wedge-shaped bricks, positioned so that they radiate from the center of curvature.

Gazebo: A structure with a roof and open sides, often located in a garden.

Gingerbread: An aesthetic style of the nineteenth century, characterized by highly decorative woodwork.

Grotto: A cave, natural or artificial, that has been incorporated into a structure, often including fountains or waterfalls.

Grouped Columns: Several columns grouped together on a single base, which act as a single structural element. See **Clustered Column**.

An old-fashioned bandstand recreates an enduring tradition in American parks. *Courtesy of Dalton Pavilions, Inc.*

Hanging post, gatepost: The post on which a gate is hinged.

Hip: The point at which two sloping roofs meet.

Hip Roof: A roof with slopes on all four sides, requiring hip joints at four corners.

A hipped roof shelters a pavilion. *Courtesy of McHale Landscape Design, Inc.*

Horseshoe arch: An arch whose greatest span occurs above its base, forming a curve greater than a semicircle. Also known as a Moorish arch.

Interlacing arcade: A row of arches set on alternating posts, such that they overlap one another.

Ionic: One of the five orders of classical architecture, typified by large **volutes** and decoration that is less ornate than that of the **Corinthian** but more detailed than the **Doric**.

Italian villa: A style of house design popular in the mid-nineteenth century in England and the United States, characterized by low-pitched roofs, square towers, and arched windows.

King-post strut: A frame formed by two inclining beams, connected at their base by a horizontal member, and further reinforced by a vertical post from the apex to the base.

Lancet window: A narrow window with a pointed arch, commonly seen in Gothic architecture.

Lattice, Latticework: An interwoven arrangement of strips or bars, forming a screen or reticulated ornament.

A pretty wood-stained wood contrasts with the white latticework on the walls of this petite two-tiered gazebo. *Courtesy of Dalton Pavilions, Inc.*

Lattice molding: A rectangular wood molding resembling latticework.

Lintel: The horizontal structural member above the opening of a window or door, which bears the load of the wall above it.

Loggia: An arcaded porch, open on at least one side and attached to a larger structure.

Molding: A decorative or structural element, often found at the base or top of a structure, which lends variety of contour to the structures it embellishes.

Moon gate: A circular opening found in classical Chinese architecture.

Mutule: A decorated block on the soffit of a **Doric** cornice.

Neoclassicism: European aesthetic movement of the eighteenth and nineteenth centuries, characterized by a strict adherence to the classical orders and sparse ornamentation.

Newel cap: An ornament at the top of a newel post. See **Newel-post**.

Newel-post: A post at the top or bottom of a staircase, supporting the handrail.

Ogee arch: A pointed, four-centered arch, with a concave lower curve and a convex upper curve.

A moon gate evokes the beauty of the Orient. *Courtesy of Trellis Structures*

Mullion: Vertical framework that separates windows, door panels, or other panels arranged in series.

Muntin: Horizontal framework, that holds glass panes within a window, though often simply decorative, arranged in series.

Muntins form arches within the glass-paned walls of a small garden house. *Courtesy of HSP Garden Buildings*

An ogee arch creates exoticism for this pointed trellis marking a pretty passageway. *Courtesy of Arboria Products*

Open-timbered: any structure leaving the timberwork exposed.

Orangery: A greenhouse for the cultivation and display of orange and other exotic trees.

Orientation: The positioning of a building or structure in relation to its surroundings.

Ornament: Any detail of shape, texture, or color.

Pagoda: A multistoried tower, traditionally of timber construction, in Japanese architecture.

Palisade: A pointed fence, constructed of posts driven into the ground.

Palladianism: A philosophy of architecture, as set forth by Italian architect Andrea Palladio, which stresses strict adherence to Roman forms, popular during the eighteenth century in England.

Panel: A raised or recessed portion of a flat surface, distinguished by its molding or decoration.

Window grid and wainscot paneling add traditional architectural details to a screened gazebo. *Courtesy of Vixen Hill Gazebos*

Panel molding: Molding which surrounds a panel, distinguishing it from the rest of the surface.

Patio: A paved outdoor area adjacent to a house.

Pavilion: A structure, often open on the sides, which is detached or semi-detached from the main building.

Pavilion roof: A roof, often of more than four sides, which is equally hipped on each side.

Pedestal: A support, traditionally composed of a base, dado, and cornice, for a statue or other item.

A pavilion in the far distance seems perched upon the nearer pedestal, dual focal points that encourage the use of all the space in between. *Courtesy of Dalton Pavilions, Inc.*

Pergola: An outdoor structure, designed to shade a walk or passageway, with an open-framed or latticework roof and open sides, on which vines or rose bushes may be trained.

A pergola is the centerpiece within a formal garden setting. *Courtesy of Trellis Structures*

Pilaster: A largely decorative, imitation pillar or pier.

Pilastrade: A row of pilasters.

Decorative pilasters with elaborate capitals stand sentinel along a handsome walkway. *Courtesy of The Gardens at Matterhorn*

Pillar: A vertical post; a column.

Pinnacle: A turret or point gracing the termination of a shaft or tower, in many cases ornamental.

Porch: A semi-enclosed area with a roof and open sides attached to a house or larger structure.

Porte cochère: A roofed structure over a driveway, protecting vehicles and their drivers from the weather.

A pergola shelters a parking area, adding ornament to an old-fashioned pea-gravel driveway. *Courtesy of Trellis Structures*

Portico: A porch whose roof is supported by columns.

Post-and-beam framing: Framing in which horizontal beams are supported by posts, as opposed to walls.

Post-and-lintel construction: Construction in which the load over openings (doors, windows, etc.) is held by a horizontal beam supported by vertical columns.

Principal beam: The main beam in a timber-framed structure.

Principal post: A corner post.

Principal rafter: A diagonal component of a roof truss, on which the **purlins** rest.

Projection: In masonry, stones set forward of the main surface of a wall. In general architecture, anything projecting from a building.

Promenade: An area designed for walking for pleasure.

A lengthy trellis forms a framework for an expansive formal garden and patio area, and creates a sheltered walkway for strolling. *Courtesy of The Gardens at Matterhorn*

Purlin: The component of a timber-framed roof which supports the **common rafters**.
Pyramidal hipped roof: see **Pavilion roof**.

Pyramid roof: A roof with four slopes rising to a single point.

Quarry-faced: Masonry stones which have been left rough-cut on the exposed face.

Queen Anne style: Style of domestic architecture popular in the 1870s and '80s in the United States and Britain; a composite of Tudor Gothic, Renaissance, and Colonial elements.

Rafter: The sloping components of a roof upon which the covering rests.

Random ashlar: Masonry in which rectangular stones are arranged to appear as though placed at random.

Random course: In masonry, a course whose height is different from that of other courses.

Random work, random range ashlar: Random masonry; rectangular stones of non-uniform height and width, fitted together without courses.

Retaining wall: A wall bearing against and resisting the force of a fill surface, frequently earth.

Ridge beam: The beam running below the ridge of a roof.

Ridgeboard: A member at the apex of a roof supporting the common rafters.

Ridge roof: A roof whose rafters meet at a ridge.

Roman arch: An arch whose curve forms a perfect half-circle, and whose members are wedge-shaped.

Romanesque architecture: Eleventh century architectural style of Western Europe, characterized by massive walls, round arches, and vaulted ceilings.

Romanesque revival: In the latter nineteenth century, the revival of Romanesque forms.

Roof: The covering of a building and its supporting structure.

Roof crest, **roof comb**: A wall running along the ridge of a roof, adding to the apparent height of a building.

Roof truss: The structure supporting a roof.

Rustic: Rough; hand-dressed masonry.

Rustic stonework creates a primitive character for a beautifully framed outlook. *Courtesy of Trellis Structures*

Rustic arch: An arch composed of irregular stones set in mortar.

Rusticated: Describing stonework with recessed joints and projecting stone faces.

Rustic brick: A brick with a rough-textured face.

Rustic slate: Shingles of non-uniform thickness, producing an irregular surface.

Rustic stone: Rough, broken stone used in rustic masonry. The stonework is generally characterized by deep grooves at joints and a rough-dressed surface.

Rustic woodwork: Woodwork incorporating unpeeled logs.

Saddle roof: A roof with one ridge and two gables.

Second Empire style: An American aesthetic and architectural style of the 1860s and 1870s, named for the French Second Empire, and characterized by high mansard roofs.

Segmental arch: A circular arch whose curve is less than a semicircle.

A gateway is crowned by a segmental arch. *Courtesy of Trellis Structures*

Semielliptical arch: An arch whose **intrados** forms a half of an ellipse.

Shaft: The part of a column between the capital and base.

Sill: The horizontal beam under a window or other frame opening.

Skirt-roof: A false, largely ornamental roof in between two stories of a building.

Soffit: The undersurface of an overhead balcony, lintel, vault, arch, etc.

A speaker is sheltered under the overhang of a roof, suspended from the soffit. *Courtesy of McHale Landscape Design, Inc.*

Springhouse: A structure housing a natural spring, often cool enough for the storage of perishable foodstuffs.

Stoop: A small porch or platform at the entrance to a building.

Story: The space between floors; one level of a building.

Stroll garden: A garden arranged so as to be viewed from a path.

Sunken garden: A garden at a lower elevation than its surroundings.

Teahouse: A Japanese garden structure used for the tea ceremony.

Theatre: A building or structure with a stage for dramatic performances.

Tie beam: In a roof, the horizontal beam connecting two rafters.

Torii: A monumental gateway to a Shinto shrine, with two pillars and a curved lintel.

Transom: A horizontal member across a window.

Trellis: An open latticework, often designed for the support of vines or other plants.

Trichila: A covered outdoor dining area, often formed with trelliswork and vines.

Angles and planes define the open work of an unusual pergola. Open woodwork will, after a few short summer seasons, be engulfed in climbing vines. *Courtesy of Dalton Pavilions, Inc.*

Tudor arch: A pointed arch with four centers of curvature, as found in much of **Tudor architecture**.

Tudor architecture: The culmination of English Perpendicular Gothic architecture, between 1485 and 1547, which was characterized by the four-centered arch.

Tufa: A volcanic building stone used often in Roman construction.

Tuscan: A simplified version of the **Doric** order, without **mutules** in the cornice.

Two-centered arch: An arch with two centers of curvature.

Two-hinged arch: An arch with hinges at each support.

Tympanum: The space enclosed by a pediment or arch, often triangular or semi-circular in shape.

Veranda, verandah: A covered porch wrapping entirely or partially around a building.

Wrought-iron work: Decorative iron-work hammered or forged into shape.

Xyst: A tree-lined walk or colonnade.

Ironwork underlies an arched gateway. *Courtesy of The Gardens at Matterhorn*

Manufacturers & Contributors

American Building Products
#2 Industrial Drive
Salem, Illinois 62881
800-851-0865
www.Americana.com

Amish Country Gazebos
340 Hostetter Road
Manheim, Pennsylvania 17565
1-800-700-1777
www.AmishGazebos.com

Arboria Products
P.O. Box 17125
Portland, Oregon 97217
800-459-8718
www.arboria.com

Dalton Pavilions, Inc.
3120 Commerce Drive
Telford, PA 18969
215-721-1492
www.daltonpavilions.com

The Gardens at Matterhorn
227 Summit Park Road
Spring Valley, NY 10977
845-354-5986
www.matterhornnursery.com

Gazebos by Leisure Designs
1957 Friendship Dr.
El Cajon, CA 92020
619-851-7608
www.leisuredesigns.net

Haddonstone
201 Heller Place
Bellmawr, NJ 08031
856-931-7011
www.haddonstone.com

HSP Garden Buildings
30a Hampstead Ave.
Mildenhall, Suffolk IP28 7AS England
0-1638 583814
www.hspgardenbuildings.com

Icon Shelter Systems, Inc.
7900 Logistic Drive Suite C
Zeeland, MI 49464
800-748-0985
www. iconshelters.com

Kleeman & Associates Design Group
350 Munroe Street
Sacramento, CA 95825
916-489-3800
www.scottlaf.com/Kleeman/

L.A. Verruni Landscaping
1357 Farmington Avenue
Pottstown, PA 19464
610-327-2622
www.verrunilandscaping.com

McHale Landscape Design, Inc.
6212 Leapley Road
Upper Marlboro, MD 20772
301-599-8300
www.mchalelandscape.com

Neals Design-Remodel
7770 East Kemper Road
Cincinnati, Ohio 45249
513-489-7700
www.neals.com

The Outdoor Greatroom Company
12400 Portland Ave. S. Suite 195
Burnsville, MN 55337
866-303-4028
www.outdoorgreatrooms.com

Trellis Structures
25 North Main Street
Templeton, MA 01438
888-285-4624
www.trellisstructures.com

Vixen Hill Cedar Products
69 E. Main Street
Elverson, PA 19520
800-423-2766
www.vixenhill.com